CW01508421

An Executive Guide to PRINCE2 Agile®

Published by TSO (The Stationery Office), part of Williams Lea, and available from:

Online
www.tsoshop.co.uk

Mail, Telephone, Fax & E-mail
TSO
PO Box 29, Norwich, NR3 1GN
Telephone orders/General enquiries: 0333 202 5070
Fax orders: 0333 202 5080
E-mail: customer.services@tso.co.uk
Textphone 0333 202 5077

TSO@Blackwell and other Accredited Agents

Cover image © istock/marty8801

Image 1.1 © istock/rusm

First edition 2017
ISBN 9780113315406
Printed in the United Kingdom for The Stationery Office
Material is FSC certified and produced using ECF pulp, sourced from fully sustainable forests.

P002883261   8/17

Contents

Foreword

Agile is a much-used term nowadays, but what does it mean?

For some it means combining flexibility with the ability to rapidly change direction. For others it is an approach used in a variety of industries to develop or revise products. Some think it is only for software development, while others see it as a way of freeing up innovation. The truth lies somewhere between, and is realized by blending the right levels of control with enough of the agile approach. To get the best out of agile usually requires a mind-set change and this can lead to more effective delivery through greater transparency, collaboration, involvement and motivation.

This executive guide to PRINCE2 Agile® uncovers the benefits of applying PRINCE2® with an agile approach to product development and delivery. The result is an organization that understands and controls its investment while also harnessing innovation. In this way the organizational energy, intellectual capacities and a sense of urgency can be brought to bear on delivering your strategy. This publication helps you to work out what you want to achieve, how to get there and how to know if you are on track, so you can gain those quick wins and build up confidence in the projects.

I recommend this guide to you as a quick way of understanding the interaction between conventional and the more agile ways of project management in order to speed up product delivery cycles while still maintaining good corporate governance over investment.

Peter Hepworth
CEO
AXELOS Global Best Practice

About AXELOS

AXELOS is a joint venture company, created in 2013 by the Cabinet Office on behalf of Her Majesty's Government in the United Kingdom and Capita plc, to manage, develop and grow the Global Best Practice portfolio. AXELOS boasts an already-enviable track record and an unmatched portfolio of globally recognized best-practice qualifications.

AXELOS is responsible for developing, enhancing and promoting a number of best-practice methodologies used globally by professionals working primarily in project, programme and portfolio management, IT service management and cyber resilience. The methodologies, including ITIL®, PRINCE2®, MSP® and the new collection of cyber resilience best-practice products, RESILIA™, are adopted in more than 150 countries to improve employees' skills, knowledge and competence in order to make both individuals and organizations work more effectively.

AXELOS is committed to nurturing best-practice communities on a global scale. In addition to globally recognized qualifications, AXELOS equips professionals with a wide range of content, templates and toolkits through its CPD-aligned AXELOS membership subscription service and its online community of practitioners and experts.

Publications

AXELOS publishes a comprehensive range of guidance, including *PRINCE2 Agile*®, which provides more detailed information on using agile with PRINCE2. Other AXELOS publications include:

- *Managing Successful Projects with PRINCE2*®
- *Directing Successful Projects with PRINCE2*®
- *Managing Successful Programmes* (MSP®)
- *Management of Portfolios* (MoP®)

- *Portfolio, Programme and Project Offices* (P3O®)
- *Management of Risk: Guidance for Practitioners* (M_o_R®)
- *Management of Value* (MoV®)
- Portfolio, Programme and Project Management Maturity Model (P3M3®)
- IT service management publications (ITIL®)
- *RESILIA™: Cyber Resilience Best Practice*.

Full details of the range of materials published under the AXELOS Global Best Practice banner, including *An Executive Guide to PRINCE2 Agile*, can be found at:

https://www.axelos.com/best-practice-solutions

If you would like to inform AXELOS of any changes that may be required to *An Executive Guide to PRINCE2 Agile*, or any other AXELOS publication, please log them at:

https://www.axelos.com/best-practice-feedback

Contact information

Full details on how to contact AXELOS can be found at:

https://www.axelos.com

For further information on qualifications and training accreditation, please visit:

https://www.axelos.com/qualifications
https://www.axelos.com/training-organization-benefits

For all other enquiries, please email:

ask@axelos.com

Acknowledgements

Author

Keith Richards

Keith is the founder and director of agileKRC, a company that has specialized in bringing the benefits of agile and Lean to organizations since the late 1990s.

Keith has more than 30 years' experience in IT and project management. He was a trainer in PRINCE2 for nearly a decade and is an accredited PRINCE2 practitioner. He is also an accredited Dynamic Systems Development Method (DSDM) advanced practitioner and trainer, and an IAF-accredited facilitator.

In 2006 he became the technical director of the DSDM Consortium and in the following year led the team that created DSDM Atern, a project-focused agile framework. Specializing in the pioneering approach of combining agile with PRINCE2, he authored the book *Agile Project Management: Running PRINCE2 projects with DSDM Atern* (TSO, 2007).

In 2010 Keith was involved in the development of Agile Project Management (AgilePM®), a ground-breaking new training course and agile qualification from APMG. He was presented with the 'Most Valuable Agile Player' award at the UK Agile Awards in 2011, in recognition of a decade of thought leadership, delivery and innovation.

In 2014 Keith was selected by AXELOS to be the lead author for *PRINCE2 Agile*, which involved an international collaboration of more than 40 people of varied experience from different backgrounds across the whole spectrum of project management and agile.

Mentor

Mike Acaster

Mike Acaster is the AXELOS PPM portfolio manager and looks after the maintenance and development of PRINCE2, MSP, MoP, M_o_R, MoV, P3O and P3M3. Mike joined AXELOS at its creation on 1 July 2013, having transferred from the Cabinet Office. He led the development of PRINCE2 Agile from inception through to product launch in June 2015. This was the first new product in the PPM portfolio since the formation of AXELOS and has created a significant amount of interest.

In August 2007, Mike was appointed to the role of PPM portfolio manager in what was then the Office of Government Commerce (OGC) and has served as project executive for the updates and developments in the Best Management Practice PPM portfolio since then. Mike was originally recruited to work on the OGC's popular Successful Delivery Toolkit but also worked on several collaborative procurement projects.

Mike joined the civil service in 2001 after a career in British Sugar's R&D centre in Norwich, where he was involved in genetic engineering, new product development and process control improvements, including an IT roll out. Prior to that, Mike led a successful career in research at several UK and American universities.

1 Introduction

1.1 About this guide

The guide is aimed at senior executives and looks at how they can benefit from using PRINCE2 Agile. After reading this guide, you should be able to understand:

- what benefits to expect from using PRINCE2 Agile (section 1.2)
- when to use PRINCE2 Agile (section 4.1)
- the key elements of PRINCE2 Agile (section 5.1)
- how to adopt PRINCE2 Agile in a sustainable way (sections 6.1, 6.2)
- the questions to ask to confirm your adoption (section 6.3).

1.2 How will PRINCE2 Agile benefit my organization?

Key message

PRINCE2 Agile helps:

- existing PRINCE2 users to work with agile methods of delivery
- agile users who want to improve governance of their projects.

PRINCE2 Agile is designed to help any individual or organization at any point on their agile journey. It is primarily targeted at organizations and practitioners who understand PRINCE2 and who want to try PRINCE2 Agile in their first-ever use of agile, but it can also be used by those who are already familiar with agile in either a basic or advanced form.

Some agile practitioners may use PRINCE2 Agile to apply extra governance and control when adapting projects to more complex situations. Even mature agile organizations can benefit from PRINCE2 Agile because it can add to their body of knowledge or provide an easy transition when engaging with customers or suppliers who are using PRINCE2.

In short, PRINCE2 Agile:

- provides detailed guidance on how to apply PRINCE2 when managing projects in an agile context where it is essential to have the basics of good project management in place
- builds on the strengths of PRINCE2 and, by doing so, illustrates that PRINCE2 is not only still relevant today, but that it is perhaps more relevant than ever
- allows your organization to use its existing PRINCE2 capability to stay current in today's ever-changing world where time is of the essence
- helps protect the quality of what is being delivered while being responsive to the needs of customers
- removes the need to start from the beginning in order to embrace agile ways of working.

Key message

If you have already adopted PRINCE2, there is no need to use an alternative approach because PRINCE2 Agile builds on the investment you have already made and takes your project management method to a new level of performance.

Consider a fighter aircraft, which is deliberately built with an unstable airframe. This instability gives it agility and allows it to change direction easily and adapt quickly to situations. However, to do this it still requires control and governance! This exemplifies PRINCE2 Agile.

Image 1.1 An agile fighter aircraft

1.3 Why do I need to change?

Today, all organizations, large and small, feel the effects of a constantly changing business environment driven by growing globalization, accelerating advances in technology and ever-demanding customer expectations. There are many examples of organizations failing because they have not recognized the need for change or have been unable to adapt quickly enough to it. Equally, organizations must be careful about the way in which they introduce change.

Many organizations around the world are adopting behaviours and techniques that are now collectively considered to be agile and this affects the way in which they deliver products and services. Organizations are turning to agile behaviours in order to stay current and competitive.

PRINCE2 Agile shows how change can be managed effectively by using the PRINCE2 management controls, and quickly and flexibly using agile behaviours and techniques. This blended approach allows agility to be introduced while following the PRINCE2 principles of good corporate governance.

2 About PRINCE2

2.1 PRINCE2 core principles

 Key message

By being based on a set of core principles, PRINCE2 is inherently agile.

PRINCE2 is a generic project management method that seeks to protect your investment in change/projects. The method is based on a set of guiding project management principles, which give PRINCE2 the flexibility to be applied to any project in any industry. The principles take into account the lessons learned from practical experience and can be summarized as:

- continued business justification: why are we doing this?
- learn from experience: draw on previous projects (our own or others)
- defined roles and responsibilities: who is responsible for what?
- manage by stages: break the work down so that it is achievable, planned, monitored and controlled
- manage by exception: delegate authority within boundaries by setting tolerances
- focus on products: define their quality and scope
- tailor to suit the project environment: do only what needs to be done for the circumstances.

Within the delivery stage(s), PRINCE2 accommodates single and multiple product releases rather than just at the end of the project or management stage.

2.2 PRINCE2 governance structure

PRINCE2 recognizes four levels of management:

● corporate or programme management (outside the project)
● directing (project board)
● managing (project manager)
● delivering (team manager).

The first level (corporate or programme management) sits above the project, while the other three levels represent the project management team. PRINCE2 concentrates on the directing and managing levels and addresses the interface with the corporate or programme management level. It is based on the concept of establishing a temporary, integrated project team drawn from across the business. The structure ensures that projects engage with suppliers and customers, and accommodates delivery teams with different skillsets. It addresses the relationship between the project manager and the team manager but it does not prescribe how the team should deliver the product described within the work package. PRINCE2 Agile deals with this latter attribute in more detail.

2.3 PRINCE2 is designed to be versatile

 Key message

A core principle of PRINCE2 is that it must be tailored to suit the organization and the individual projects on which it is used.

It is essential to ensure that your view of PRINCE2 is not affected by any stereotyping in the sense that PRINCE2 is a 'traditional' approach to project management. Many in the agile community attempt to promote or sell the idea of agile by contrasting it against traditional approaches. They define these as bureaucratic, document-driven and Waterfall-based, using a command and control style of project management.

Although PRINCE2 does have a long and established tradition in the field of project management, it is a versatile and generic method that should be applied and configured appropriately. PRINCE2 can be used in an agile or more serial way and that is your choice. But to characterize PRINCE2 as being inherently a Waterfall approach is fundamentally incorrect.

 What types of project can use PRINCE2?

PRINCE2 is a generic project management method that has been successfully adapted for IT-based implementations, the financial sector, business and support services, engineering, manufacturing and many other industries.

A PRINCE2 project is broken down into management stages that can be configured however you want; in an agile context, these management stages would typically be set up to deliver sets of features structured as one or more releases. PRINCE2 projects can readily be designed to support the agile frequent-release, early-delivery approach.

Evidence for the flexibility of PRINCE2 is in its international adoption. It is used in more than 150 countries across the globe by private and public sector organizations, both large and small.

How does PRINCE2 Agile view management stages?

A management stage is, in effect, a high-level timebox and will usually contain one or more lower-level timeboxes such as releases or sprints. The concept of a PRINCE2 management stage does not have an exact equivalent that is commonly used in agile.

Further research

As long as the principles are followed, PRINCE2 can be adapted for projects of every scale, from low-budget, short-term to complex, long-term and high-budget undertakings. See also the 2016 PRINCE2® Report at https://www.axelos.com/2016-prince2-report [accessed 10 May 2017].

3 About agile

3.1 What problems does agile seek to address?

The world has changed dramatically in recent years with the increased use of technology and the establishment of the internet as an essential part of our everyday lives. This has led to a change in how organizations deliver products and services. Delivery needs to be faster, more responsive and more in tune with the requirements of more demanding customers.

Historically, project management has suffered from these common problems:

- late delivery and even non-delivery
- constantly changing requirements
- costly overruns
- not delivering what the customer wanted or needed
- poor quality
- high ownership costs
- limited future-proofing.

3.2 How does agile address these problems?

In the late 1990s, many flexible and adaptive frameworks and approaches came into existence to address the need to work in a different way. This in turn created the agile movement that aimed to counter the common problems by thinking differently. And some of this thinking was *very* different.

Key message

Agile addresses common project problems by:

- being time-focused (e.g. by timeboxing)
- allowing for change and embracing it
- fixing resources and the associated costs
- working iteratively and incrementally to allow an accurate solution to emerge
- protecting quality by 'checking as you go' and not falling behind
- maximizing the amount of value that is ultimately delivered to the customer.

The most fundamental difference was to work quickly, over short time intervals, in an iterative and incremental way in order to deliver something of use as early as possible. The product or service would then evolve in this way over time. This was in direct contrast to the Waterfall approach where delivery would take place towards the end of the project and often resulted in big bang implementations. The advantage of the agile way of working is that not only can something be delivered quickly but the corresponding feedback about what is delivered is gathered quickly too.

However, to work in this way requires more than a different process. It requires a different mind-set, the appropriate techniques in order to make agile happen, and the establishment of behaviours that allow an organization to adapt and respond more easily. This new agile approach seeks to harness behaviours such as collaboration, transparency and self-organization.

In tandem with these behaviours, techniques such as timeboxing and requirements prioritization ensure frequent deliveries that give a clear measure of progress and clarity on fitness for purpose.

3.3 What are the benefits of using agile?

The advantage of using agile is that it provides organizations with what they need to flourish in today's environment in the form of early learnings, reduced risk and the faster delivery of benefits.

By breaking down a complex problem into smaller chunks, it is quicker to get customer feedback and therefore stay on track. When things are smaller they progress faster and it is easier to make many small adjustments in order to give all stakeholders confidence in what is happening and deliver a more accurate solution. The ability to fail fast is at the heart of this. If you are going in the wrong direction, you need to know this as quickly as possible. Going in the right direction by delivering some, or most, of what was needed *early*, as opposed to all of it at a later date, can be the difference between success and failure.

3.4 Is agile 'problem-free'?

Agile is not a simple panacea to the well-known project management problems. As the number of success stories about agile increases every day, so too do the failures.

Self-organizing and empowered teams working under light governance can lead to success or failure depending on how the project is executed. Agile reduces many of the risks associated with Waterfall projects but has risks of its own. There is, therefore, a need to incorporate appropriate governance that has flexibility in order to compensate for these risks when running a project. PRINCE2 Agile seeks to address this.

It is ironic that agile has no clear definition that everyone can sign up to, despite having been adopted by so many people. The Agile Manifesto is the closest but as this is not actively maintained, some elements may not reflect current thinking. In order to address common project problems, the drive to 'go agile' has gathered pace, but with this has emerged a new problem: that of 'fragile agile'. Symptoms of this can be:

- poor design
- rushed testing and quality checking
- a never-ending job with something always left to be done
- cost and timescales out of control
- customer expectations not met
- non-existent documentation
- non-compliance to standards
- lack of appropriate training.

These are typical side-effects of poorly implemented agile. Frequently, the hype surrounding agile has led to many disappointments because what was promised has resulted in something that was far worse than what would have been delivered using existing working practices.

When using agile, there is a need to invest in the areas that make it work. This includes ensuring that the right behaviours are taking place, that expectations are being managed, that a strong relationship is being fostered with the customer and, above all, that a clear level of control exists where everyone knows who is doing what.

Further research

Appendix E of *PRINCE2 Agile* summarizes the Agile Manifesto, while Scrum is described in Appendix H.

4 Introduction to PRINCE2 Agile

Key message

PRINCE2 Agile gives very clear guidance on how the right levels of management and control can be applied to an agile working environment to produce a 'whole that is greater than the sum of the parts'.

4.1 When to use PRINCE2 Agile

When looking at whether PRINCE2 Agile will benefit an organization, consideration has to be given to the type of work that is undertaken and whether agile is already being used. If agile is only being used for ongoing, business as usual (BAU) work, then this limits the range of where agile can be applied. Agile is equally at home in a project context, and this is where PRINCE2 Agile can be used as it shows how to apply agile to projects.

You cannot take the basic fundamentals of agile that apply on BAU work and use them in a project without making significant changes. The most popular agile method is Scrum. It is excellent at evolving an existing product and, although it is not a project management framework, it can be used on many projects.

PRINCE2 Agile contains all the elements needed to leverage agile ways of working in a project context. Although you cannot use Scrum to *run* a project, you can still use it *on* a project. PRINCE2 Agile shows you how to incorporate this and other well-known frameworks such as Kanban and Lean Startup.

4.2 The benefits of applying PRINCE2 to agile working

PRINCE2 is very strong at the project direction and project management levels. It is the most widely used project management method in the world. Agile is very strong at the product delivery level as epitomized by methods such as Scrum and Kanban. Therefore, to get the best of both methodologies there is a need to create a synergy or a blend, and this is what PRINCE2 Agile provides.

PRINCE2 and agile will not operate effectively if they are implemented independently of each other on the same project. They need to be woven together so that the strengths of PRINCE2 can permeate the agile ways of working where needed, and conversely the agile ways of working need to infiltrate the higher levels of project management and direction (see Figure 4.1).

4.3 Why should my organization care about PRINCE2 Agile?

Any organization in today's world needs to have a clear understanding of PRINCE2 Agile and the role it can play. In the past, agile was regarded by some as a niche area and the preserve of IT or technology, but nowadays agile thinking is being applied to everything from nuclear submarines to marketing campaigns. Working and thinking in an agile way is BAU for many and, therefore, senior personnel in any organization are ultimately responsible for how effectively agile is utilized.

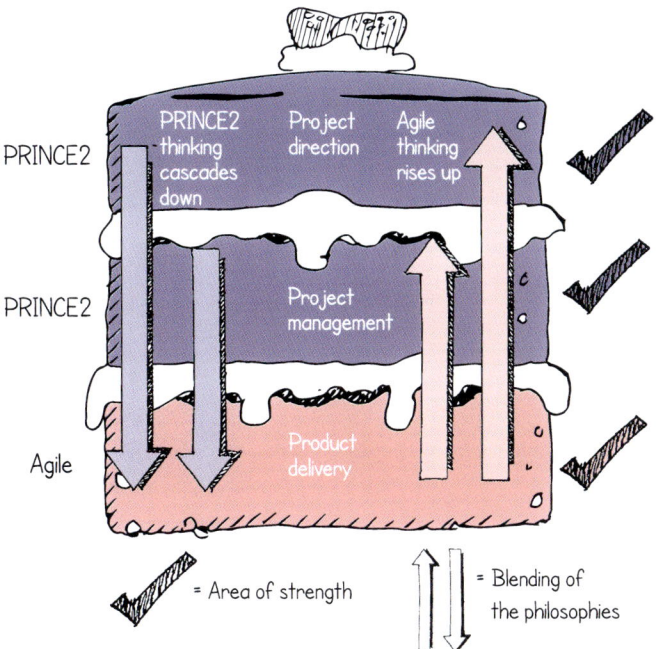

Figure 4.1 Blending PRINCE2 and agile together

It is essential that PRINCE2 Agile is sponsored and promoted from the top down to release its full potential, and this attitude needs to be sustained in senior management. If agile is introduced into an organization at the delivery level and then spreads virally, the results can be chaotic.

Key message

As with PRINCE2, PRINCE2 Agile is tailorable for the organization and the specific needs of a project.

4.4 What is expected of me in a project context?

The previous section described the wider implications of how senior executives need to perceive PRINCE2 Agile because its introduction usually requires a cultural change that affects the whole organization.

However, senior executives will need to do more than this: they also have to behave and act in an agile way when they hold important senior positions such as project executive. They need to back up their words with actions.

The role of the people giving direction to a project is vital and this is also true in an agile environment. They have to set clear boundaries and provide the appropriate level of governance in order to allow for the required degrees of autonomy and self-organization that agile demands. An ethos of command and control will stifle and perhaps kill the agile mind-set. A project board in an agile context will be clear on the need to get 'from A to B' but the project manager and the delivery teams will work out how this is best achieved if they are appropriately empowered and trusted.

PRINCE2 Agile, in the same way as other agile approaches, focuses on what is being delivered and its quality and acceptance criteria. The people involved in giving direction to a project need to think in this way. They must protect and motivate self-organizing teams and work collaboratively with the teams.

An indication of the 'agile friendliness' of senior executives is seen in how they relate to the project teams. Is reporting carried out with high levels of ceremony and documentation or is there a 'light touch'? A highlight report can be pulled from the information radiator in a team room (see Figure 4.2) but the project board needs to understand enough about agile to be able to do this. This would be a typical agile behaviour that builds on the transparency created by the agile way of working.

Figure 4.2 An example of an information radiator

5 What is PRINCE2 Agile?

Key message

PRINCE2 Agile:

- works for all types of project, not just IT
- can be used with any agile method but focuses on the most popular, those of Scrum and Kanban
- recognizes that accommodating agile behaviours is key to success
- includes new tools that help:
  - assess how suitable a project may be for agile working
  - define the tolerances for agile working.

PRINCE2 Agile describes how to configure and tune PRINCE2 so that it can be used in the most effective way when combined with agile ways of working.

There are some very important things to understand about PRINCE2 Agile and the assumptions upon which it is based. There are eight 'guidance points':

- PRINCE2 is already enabled for agile.
- PRINCE2 is not a traditional Waterfall project management approach.
- PRINCE2 Agile is for any project not just IT projects.

- 'IT-only' frameworks are mentioned but not extensively.
- Agile is more than just Scrum.
- Scrum and Kanban are the most popular agile methods.
- PRINCE2 Agile sees agile as a family of behaviours, frameworks, concepts and techniques.
- Agile is not an all-or-nothing condition. It is a question of degree.

PRINCE2 Agile is an extension to PRINCE2. It provides guidance on how to configure and tailor PRINCE2 to run in an agile context. In some situations it may not be possible to go fully agile. There isn't anything in PRINCE2 that needs to be removed or switched off to make it suitable for agile. Even though PRINCE2 is a traditional approach, since its revision in 2009 it has become agile-enabled because it focuses on the staged delivery of product(s) of agreed quality.

Agile is often seen as the preserve of IT. Most of the available guidance is described in an IT context even though PRINCE2 and PRINCE2 Agile can support projects in any environment. Although PRINCE2 Agile does reference IT occasionally (as this is where the heritage of agile is), it can be applied to any project, not just IT.

Another guidance point upon which PRINCE2 Agile is based is the Scrum framework. Even though Scrum is the most popular agile framework and has shaped a lot of agile thinking, it is important not to limit the view of agile to just Scrum. Scrum is agile, but agile is more than Scrum.

Having said that, it is essential that any guidance on how to direct and manage a project in an agile context needs to state clearly where Scrum, and also Kanban, fit in. PRINCE2 Agile focuses on these two approaches above all others.

Key message

PRINCE2 Agile does not categorize projects as being either 'agile' or 'not agile': it is more concerned with the degree to which they have adopted agile.

The final two guidance points underpin the need to understand agile and how it should be applied. PRINCE2 Agile sees agile as a collection of various practices and not just one framework or belief system (see section 5.1). On any project you will be able to use agile in some form. Some contexts will lend themselves to being highly suitable for agile, whereas others may be less so.

5.1 The key elements of PRINCE2 Agile

5.1.1 How PRINCE2 Agile views agile

PRINCE2 Agile takes a big picture view of agile (see Figure 5.1). Incorporated in this view is the need to promote specific behaviours that underpin working practices with concepts such as prioritization and incremental delivery.

Many people see agile in other ways. Some see it as just a set of behaviours or a mind-set. Others consider it to be a framework. Many people practising agile today are simply using a toolbox of agile techniques.

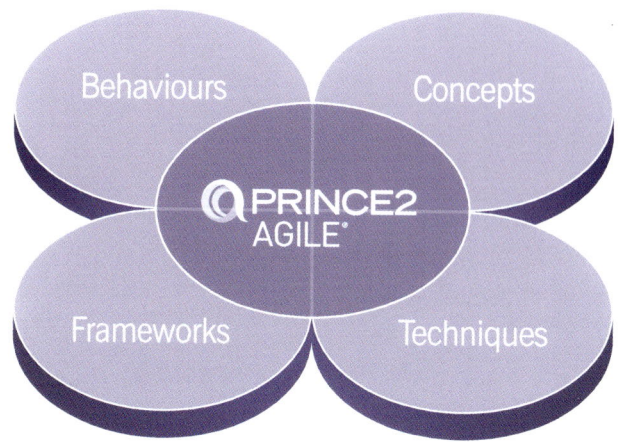

Figure 5.1 How PRINCE2 Agile sees agile

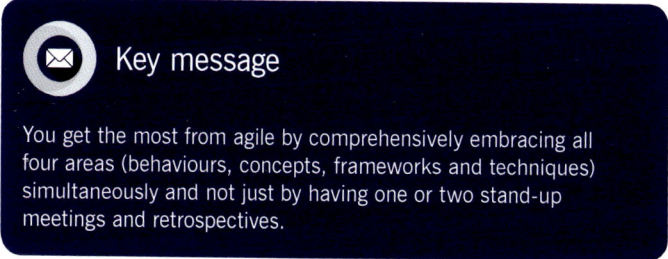

Key message

You get the most from agile by comprehensively embracing all four areas (behaviours, concepts, frameworks and techniques) simultaneously and not just by having one or two stand-up meetings and retrospectives.

5.1.2 PRINCE2 Agile: what to fix and what to flex?

The iron triangle

When describing project management, many people will, at some point, refer to the competing considerations of time, cost and quality. This is often referred to as the 'iron triangle' and is a common feature of many project management training courses. However, the triangle often varies in what it is trying to describe and may include other constraints such as scope.

PRINCE2 identifies six aspects of a project that have some degree of flexibility and to which tolerances can be applied: time, cost, scope, quality, risks and benefits. Some of these aspects are more relevant to specific situations than others; this determines which aspects to fix or flex and what tolerance levels to apply.

No more triangles – the PRINCE2 Agile hexagon

The best way to show how all six aspects of PRINCE2 behave in an agile context is in the form of a hexagon (see Figure 5.2). This illustrates how the competing constraints on a project are to be set and managed in an agile context. In simple terms, it explains what to fix and what to flex when using PRINCE2 Agile.

Working in an agile way is often seen as a complete reversal of what has traditionally occurred. In the past, it was quite normal to manage time and cost while ensuring that the appropriate level of quality was achieved. Agile is different. The use of timeboxing, with its immovable deadlines and stable teams, means that there is little to 'manage' in terms of time and cost (in the form of resources). The variables in this context typically focus on what is actually being delivered. In other words, it is the scope (in the form of requirements, features or functions) that is managed. This in turn is how agile achieves the appropriate level of quality, while at the same time meeting deadlines.

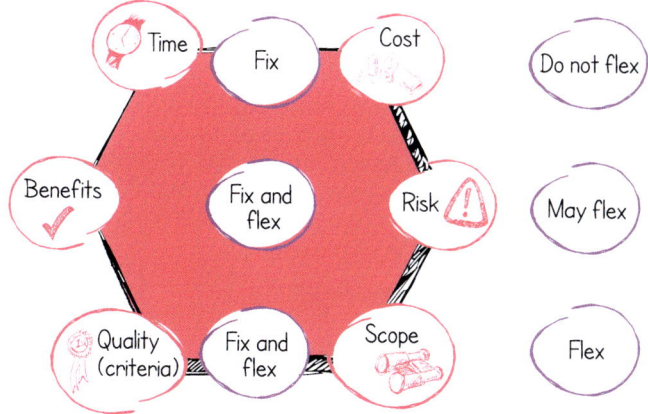

Figure 5.2 The PRINCE2 Agile hexagon

Tolerances: the key to using the hexagon

One of the most powerful features of PRINCE2 is the use of tolerances that enable a project to be managed by exception. The project board and the project manager set these, thereby empowering the teams and individuals to get on with their work until the tolerances are forecast to go outside their limits.

The hexagon in Figure 5.2 shows how tolerances could be set when using PRINCE2 in an agile context. In this project environment there is no flexibility on time or cost. Every timebox at any level (e.g. a two-week sprint or a three-month stage) has zero tolerance; in other words, time is fixed so that the project manager cannot move any deadlines. If a deadline needs to be moved, then an exception condition must be raised with the project board. Likewise, cost has a zero tolerance level, so that adding resources to speed things up over the short term will also cause an exception.

PRINCE2 Agile is flexible with respect to the tolerances it gives to the scope (and the corresponding quality criteria). In other words, when using PRINCE2 in an agile context, it is assumed that not everything will be delivered but that tolerances will be set to describe what can be allowed and at what point an exception needs to happen (e.g. when too much has been de-scoped).

Tolerances may be set for benefits and risk as well to suit the needs of the project, but the main point of the hexagon is to illustrate that time and cost/resources are fixed, and that scope and quality criteria are flexible.

Further research

Chapter 6 of *PRINCE2 Agile* provides a fuller explanation of managing tolerances, and what to fix and flex.

5.1.3 Distinguishing between quality criteria and the quality level

It is very important to understand that being flexible with quality criteria is not the same as being flexible with the overall quality level. A camera provides a good example of three possible quality criteria:

- The shutter **must** operate at $-5°C$.
- The shutter **should** operate at $-20°C$.
- The shutter **could** operate at $-35°C$.

If a deadline needs to be met for the delivery of the camera and dropping the 'could' criterion enables this to be achieved, it does not mean that the overall quality level described by the customer's quality expectations has been compromised. In effect, the opposite has happened because the minimum required quality level has been protected.

How tolerances are used, in the form of what to fix and what to flex, is essential to configuring PRINCE2 appropriately to run in an agile context. The rationale for using the tolerances in this way is based around five targets, as described by PRINCE2 Agile.

5.1.4 The five targets: the thinking behind the hexagon

The drivers and the thinking behind the PRINCE2 Agile hexagon relate to the need to achieve a desirable outcome for a project, which involves creating good habits and also accepting the realities of projects in today's fast-moving and uncertain world.

 Key message

The five targets that provide the case for PRINCE2 Agile flexible working are:

- be on time and hit deadlines
- protect the level of quality
- embrace change
- keep teams stable
- accept that the customer does not need everything.

Be on time and hit deadlines

Being on time has many significant advantages. Avoiding cost overruns, being able to plan and schedule resources, and delivering something when the customer wants it are by no means trivial. On top of this is the effect it has on the many stakeholders as it gives them confidence and builds a positive reputation. This target is vital to keeping agile in control at all times. It could be said to be quite brutal because if you are failing to hit a deadline, it is highlighting that all is not well with the project. It can force fast termination of a failing project.

Protect the level of quality

When projects run into difficulty, it is often quality that suffers because quality checking, documentation and design are compromised in the rush to make up for lost time. In PRINCE2 Agile, the scope and quality criteria are flexed so that what is delivered is well tested, well documented and well designed. The key point here is that lower-priority work is de-scoped to keep the project on time and at the correct level of quality for the 'must have' requirements.

Embrace change

Agile is regarded as being change-friendly and it is assumed that thinking and behaving in an agile way are more likely to achieve an accurate solution. The customer usually knows roughly what they want, but rarely do they know exactly. Being open to change is therefore seen as an advantage, although PRINCE2 Agile highlights the importance of having the 'right kind of change'. Change to the detail is fine, but if the change affects the overall vision of a piece of work, then this needs to be escalated to the project board.

Keep teams stable

In a complex environment, trying to speed up progress by adding members to a team can be counter-productive in the short term. This can be explained by the time it takes to bring new members up to speed and the effect it has on team dynamics. The very nature of agile is to work in short time intervals; therefore it is important to have the right team in place for the timebox to work. Changing the composition of a team by adding more people should be avoided, and the PRINCE2 Agile mechanism to prevent this from happening is to set the cost tolerance for a timebox to zero.

Accept that the customer does not need everything

PRINCE2 Agile highlights the point that when a project is set up, the customer may say they want everything, but the reality is that some things are more important than others, such as being on time and delivering an accurate product. Therefore this 'reality' is built in as a target and is a key reason why a project can focus its attention on areas that are vital, as opposed to 'nice to have' items that may not even get used. A good example of this is the number of programs in a washing machine that are hardly ever used.

5.2 The PRINCE2 principles and agile behaviours

The seven PRINCE2 principles (see section 2.1) are immutable in the sense that they cannot be tailored or adjusted in any way. Many of these principles capture the very essence of agile.

However, when using PRINCE2 in an agile environment, additional factors need to be considered in order for agile to function as effectively as possible. PRINCE2 Agile refers to these as behaviours (see Figure 5.3). They are not specifically covered in PRINCE2 because it can support any style of leadership and management, whereas the style of working in an agile context needs to support a certain ethos and culture.

5.2.1 The five PRINCE2 Agile behaviours

Transparency

A very simple and effective way to create more control and understanding on a project is to make it as visible as possible. Such visible displays are

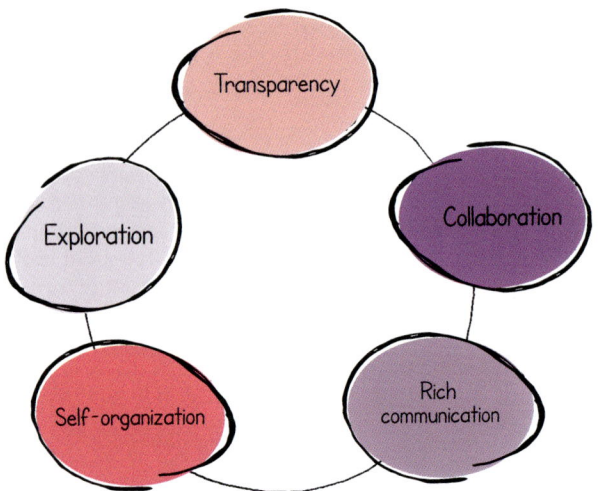

Figure 5.3 PRINCE2 Agile behaviours

usually referred to as 'information radiators' (Figure 4.2) or 'big visible charts' (BVCs), but to be effective they must be truthful and trusted by all.

Collaboration

A critical element for the success of agile working is a high level of collaboration as opposed to 'siloed' working. Trading requirements and adjusting plans need cooperation as opposed to negotiation.

Rich communication

Communication problems are often cited as issues. Agile creates communication-rich environments with plenty of visualization, demonstrations, team interaction, and a desire to reduce documentation.

Self-organization

Self-organization is key to working in an agile way. It is important to allow individuals to determine how they work and plan together as opposed to following someone else's plan to which they have had little input.

Exploration

Exploration is all about trying to uncover what the customer really wants. The more that is proactively uncovered during a project, the easier it will be to meet the customer's expectations.

5.3 Tailoring the PRINCE2 themes and processes

PRINCE2 Agile explains how to configure the seven themes and seven processes of PRINCE2 in an agile context. The guidance explains what adjustments to make and how they will look in real life. It shows how to handle different levels of rigour and formality, and how to change existing working practices so that they function effectively in an agile setting.

The seven PRINCE2 themes are:

- Business case
- Organization
- Quality
- Plans
- Risk
- Change
- Progress.

The seven PRINCE2 processes are:

- Starting up a project
- Directing a project
- Initiating a project
- Controlling a stage
- Managing product delivery
- Managing a stage boundary
- Closing a project.

PRINCE2 Agile shows how to tailor the themes and processes of PRINCE2 to take advantage of the benefits of agile delivery while maintaining the integrity of PRINCE2 management. In this way PRINCE2 Agile remains true to the principles of PRINCE2.

5.4 The PRINCE2 Agile focus areas

 Key message

The focus areas that help optimize the use of PRINCE2 Agile are as follows:

- the Agilometer (assessing the suitability of agile)
- definition and prioritization of requirements
- rich communication
- frequent releases
- creating contracts when using agile.

Although it is important to understand that there is nothing in PRINCE2 that needs to be removed or switched off, there are additional areas of guidance included in PRINCE2 Agile. These are referred to as focus areas and they provide an extra level of support that enables PRINCE2 to run successfully in an agile context.

5.4.1 The Agilometer

The Agilometer is used to assess relevant prevailing project characteristics (see Figure 5.4). It gives a good idea of how successful agile working may be for a given project, or how the project environment may need to

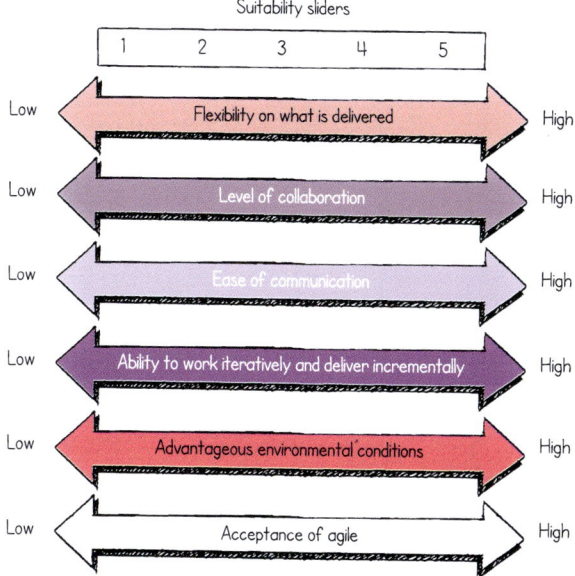

Figure 5.4 The Agilometer

change to make agile more appropriate. PRINCE2 Agile does not treat a project as being 'agile' or 'not agile'; instead it sees the project in terms of the degree to which it is able to adopt agile. The Agilometer can be used to validate the amount of agile used.

The Agilometer is a starting point for any project and helps to clarify the conditions that are favourable for working in an agile way (e.g. a high level of collaboration) and those that are less favourable (e.g. not easy to work iteratively and deliver incrementally). The slider values (1: low to 5: high) are indicative and are intended to identify areas for improvement, rather than accurate scores. The results are then used to look at the risk areas that can be reduced or mitigated against.

The Agilometer is a helpful support tool when deciding whether to use agile or a more traditional approach in a specific project environment.

Further reading

Part III of *PRINCE2 Agile* covers the areas of focus for PRINCE2 Agile and includes a comprehensive explanation of the Agilometer.

5.4.2 Definition and prioritization of requirements

This focus area looks at how to define, prioritize and manage requirements, which represent the 'currency' that is used on a project in an agile setting. Defining a requirement means describing it so that it is clearly understood and flexible enough to help with prioritization. PRINCE2 Agile describes the popular technique of user story writing, along with best-practice tips and how to avoid making classic mistakes. It also shows how to decompose requirements, define non-functional requirements and counter the claim that they are all 'must haves'.

5.4.3 Rich communication

Shifting communication to the clearer channels of face-to-face and visualization reduces the amount of effort needed to convey meaning through forms such as email. 'A picture paints a thousand words' and several approaches exist to facilitate high-speed, high-quality communication, many of which are standard agile techniques. One such example is the use of facilitated workshops where a correctly executed event can create outputs quickly and give ownership to the people who created it. This will not happen by itself and needs to be tailored to the project environment.

5.4.4 Frequent releases

There are several advantages to releasing something of use as frequently as possible; these include early learnings and early delivery of benefits. The agile way of working sees frequent releases as an essential element of planning a project. The more releases into operational use the better, but this still needs to be planned carefully to ensure business continuity in the operational environment. There is a strong focus on this concept as it may be possible to deliver something that proves very early on whether the business case is viable.

5.4.5 Creating contracts when using agile

PRINCE2 Agile includes guidance in this area because contracts are often cited as being difficult when using agile. Traditionally contracts are drawn up to define in advance precisely what will be delivered; often they provide an adversarial framework where one party or another is responsible if things go wrong. The agile concept of emergence (where detailed work is deferred until later in the project) contrasts with this approach, and agile contracts need to consider factors such as setting requirements at a higher level, and agreeing the level of engagement needed from the customer.

6 Adopting PRINCE2 Agile in an organization

PRINCE2 organizations that are looking to develop their agile capability, or even to begin to adopt agile, should see this as a journey. It will not happen overnight: no matter how small or large an organization is, it will take several months, possibly even years.

When deciding which approach to adopt, you need to understand:

- where you are
- what problems you are trying to solve
- how your organization reacts to change, which will help plan for improvements.

These elements should be kept in mind when deciding which project management approach to adopt for the whole organization or to use on an individual project.

6.1 Your PRINCE2 Agile destination

Before starting the journey, you must decide on your destination: why are you looking to adopt PRINCE2 Agile? Section 3.3 described how agile can provide some project delivery benefits. These include:

- greater control over investment decisions, project start up and closure
- better responsiveness to customer requirements
- greater use of best practice: it is what many good project managers already do
- stronger alignment across all projects within the organization.

What additional benefits could I get from PRINCE2 Agile?

You may be looking to introduce:

- greater empowerment
- better governance (e.g. in a 'fragile agile' environment)
- agile techniques and greater flexibility into a traditional project management environment.

It is important to define a clear vision of where you want to be with PRINCE2 Agile.

6.2 The journey

Each organization will be different but there are some elements that will be common for every journey. These are as follows:

- Know your project environment

  - Understand where you and your organization are in relation to current project practices, as well as people's attitudes to that position.

  - Understand your organization's attitude towards PRINCE2 Agile and agile in general:

    consider appropriate awareness and training courses, including PRINCE2 Agile

    engage in community discussions about introducing agile into your organization undertake an Agilometer assessment, perhaps using your project management office (PMO) or centre of excellence (COE).

- Be prepared
  - See this as any other business change exercise that:
    - needs to be planned
    - requires a change in organizational culture to reflect desired agile project attitudes and behaviours
    - requires an understanding that the solution may not be obvious at the start of the project but will emerge as the project progresses
    - requires a change in leadership style.
  - Find someone to champion the changes, who should:
    - exhibit many of the agile characteristics (open, communicative, empowering, collaborative)
    - be motivated to make the introduction succeed.
  - Make sure there is an agreed set of benefits you are trying to achieve.
  - If you have a PMO or COE, make use of it. You will need to ensure that:
    - PRINCE2 Agile and agile techniques feature as a specialist skillset within your PMO or COE
    - the PMO or COE has the capabilities to tailor PRINCE2 to get the optimal blend of PRINCE2 and agile for your organization.
- Keep on track to your destination
  - Take small steps as it will not happen overnight:
    - Target adoption in part of your organization then expand to other parts as appropriate

Focus adoption on targeted pilot projects to build up confidence; demonstrate early/quick wins; and generate an appetite for the change and PRINCE2 Agile.

● Build on the successes and learn from the failures of the pilot projects to develop a project culture that enables agile working.

● Regularly review your progress:

so that you can make adjustments to keep on the path to your destination

against the agreed set of benefits.

6.3 How is your agile journey going?

You will want assurance that the journey is going well and there are some key questions you should be asking:

● Is collaboration happening?

● Is communication effective?

● Is it easy to see that the project is under control?

● Is everyone on the project 'thinking agile'?

● Are deliveries happening frequently?

● Is the customer fully engaged?

● Has something of benefit already been delivered?

● Are deadlines fixed?

● Is planning a team-based activity?

● Is the project board empowering people?

Chapter 5 covers some of the answers to these questions. These include the areas of focus for PRINCE2 Agile (the Agilometer, requirements, rich communication, frequent releases and contracts), project organization and behaviours, what to fix and flex, and how you approach planning.

Further reading

PRINCE2 Agile gives guidance to help you check the suitability of your project environment for using agile and PRINCE2 together and helps you to create the right balance of control and agility for your projects. The guide includes a detailed health check so that you can test that you are getting the benefits you were expecting.

6.4 One last thing: beware of prejudice

It would be understandable to think that bringing more control and governance into the agile domain could prove counter-productive and stifle the creativity and benefits of agile working. However, PRINCE2 Agile represents a partnership that is based on the opposite view – that control and governance allow agile to be used in more situations, such as those involving multiple teams or complex environments.

Glossary

exception

A situation where it can be forecast that there will be a deviation beyond the tolerance levels agreed between the project manager and project board (or between the project board and corporate, programme management or the customer).

executive

The individual with overall responsibility for ensuring that a project meets its objectives and delivers the projected benefits. This individual should ensure that the project maintains its business focus, that it has clear authority and that the work, including risks, is actively managed. The executive is the chair of the project board. He or she represents the customer and is responsible for the business case.

information radiator

A general term used to describe the use of walls or boards containing information that can be readily accessed by people working on the project. It can contain any information, although it would typically show such things as work to do and how work is progressing.

Kanban board

A tool used in Kanban to visually display the work in the system (or timebox). It is usually made up of a series of columns and possibly rows where work items move from left to right as they move through various states in order to be completed.

Lean

An approach that focuses on improving processes by maximizing value through eliminating waste (such as wasted time and wasted effort).

manage by exception

A technique by which variances from plan that exceed a pre-set control limit are escalated for action – for example, where spends exceed budget by 10 per cent.

management stage

The section of a project that the project manager is managing on behalf of the project board at any one time, at the end of which the project board will wish to review progress to date, the state of the project plan, the business case and risks, and the next stage plan, in order to decide whether to continue with the project.

project

A temporary organization that is created for the purpose of delivering one or more business products according to an agreed business case.

project management

The planning, delegating, monitoring and control of all aspects of the project, and the motivation of those involved, to achieve the project objectives within the expected performance targets for time, cost, quality, scope, benefits and risks.

release

The set of products in a handover. The contents of a release are managed, tested and deployed as a single entity.

In PRINCE2 Agile, a release is typically a container for more than one low-level timebox (e.g. a sprint). This is not always the case as the act of releasing features into operational use may happen more regularly (e.g. after each sprint or several times during a sprint). The term 'deployment' is sometimes used in agile and has a similar meaning, although it is not used in PRINCE2 Agile.

requirement

A term to describe what a product does and/or how it will do it. A requirement can be written in the form of a user story if desired and will exist with other requirements in the form of a list.

Scrum

An iterative timeboxed approach to product delivery that is described as 'a framework within which people can address complex adaptive problems, while productively and creatively delivering products of the highest possible value'.

sprint

A fixed timeframe (typically of 2–4 weeks) for creating selected features from the backlog.

stage

See management stage.

timebox

A finite period of time during which work is carried out to achieve a goal or meet an objective. The deadline should not be moved, as the method of managing a timebox is to prioritize the work inside it. At a low level a timebox will last a matter of days or weeks (e.g. a sprint). Higher-level timeboxes act as aggregated timeboxes and contain lower-level timeboxes.

tolerance

The permissible deviation above and below a plan's target for time and cost without escalating the deviation to the next level of management. There may also be tolerance levels for quality, scope, benefits and risk. Tolerance is applied at project, management stage and team levels.

value

The benefits delivered in proportion to the resources put into acquiring them.

Waterfall method

A development approach that is linear and sequential, with distinct goals for each phase of development.

After a phase of development has been completed, the development proceeds to the next phase and earlier phases are not revisited (hence the analogy that water flowing down a mountain cannot go back).